This book belongs to:

_____

LEARN about PetCare

with Bearific®

KATELYN LONAS

- Pet Care -

Learn how to care for 28 different pets to maintain their health and well-being while also providing them with a safe, comfortable, and loving environment for them to grow in.

- Bearded Dragons -

Bearded dragons are popular reptile pets that are known for their distinct and unique appearance. In general, bearded dragons are curious, friendly, gentle, and very responsive to people. They can be found in a variety of colors, like orange, red, and shades of brown.

Basic Needs

- reptile enclosure
- food, water, and treats
- substrate
- food and water bowl
- space to exercise
- appropriate lighting and heating
- objects to promote natural behaviors

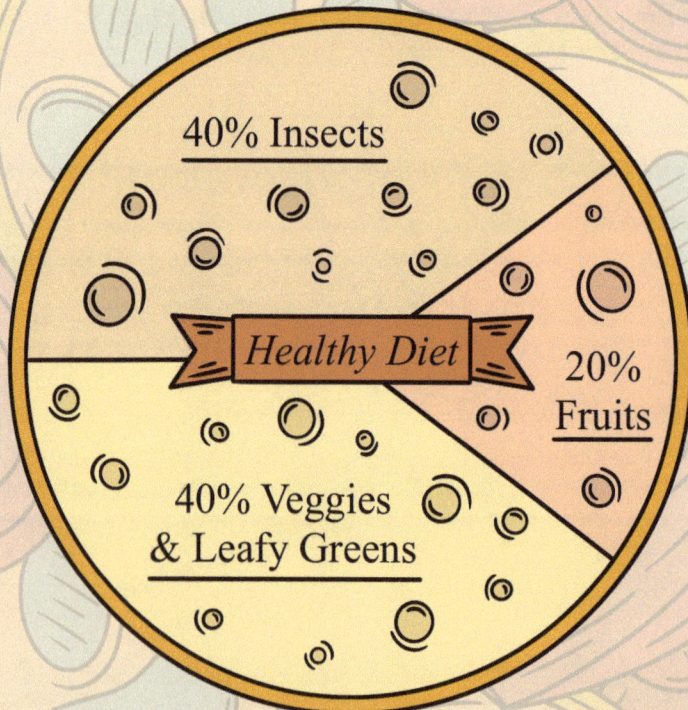

40% Insects

Healthy Diet

20% Fruits

40% Veggies & Leafy Greens

- *Home* -

A bearded dragon's perfect environment will need a spacious cage that will allow them room to move around and explore. Remember, as your pet grows, it's important to upgrade your cage to fit their appropriate size. When choosing your bearded dragon's cage, avoid mesh and wire cages because they don't hold heat effectively and can cause injuries. While setting up the cage, provide a basking area with a heat lamp that maintains higher temperatures during the day. Be sure to install lighting to mimic natural sunlight and include lots of hiding spots like caves or half-logs for your bearded dragon.

Friends:
Bearded dragons can be social animals, but they are often territorial and don't usually seek social interaction. However, housing multiple bearded dragons is a possibility as long as there is enough space and resources for each one.

Did you know?

- bearded dragons have the ability to swim and can hold their breath for up to 2 minutes
- bearded dragons are native to Australia
- bearded dragons can change colors and regrow their teeth

- Cats -

Cats are low-maintenance and independent pets. The majority of them naturally know how to use the litter box. Although a cat's personality is known to vary depending on its breed, cats make very affectionate pets. There are more than 40 species of cats.

Basic Needs

- cat bed
- food, water, and treats
- grooming products such as shampoo, nail clippers, and a brush
- food and water bowl
- litter box
- cat tower
- scratching post

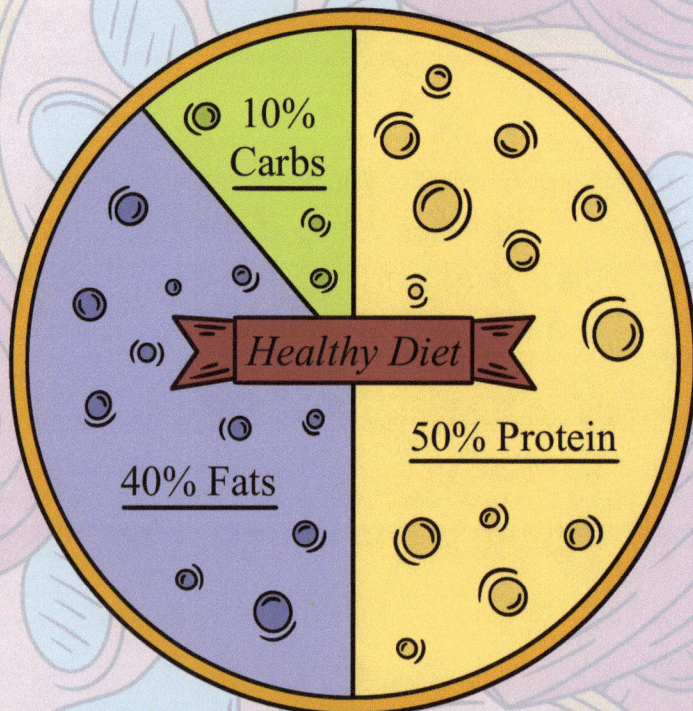

10%
Carbs

Healthy Diet

50% Protein

40% Fats

- Home -

Each cat is unique and has their own personality, so be sure to adjust their environment accordingly. Some cats enjoy being inside, while others prefer to be outside. Indoor cats need enough space for them to move around, exercise, and climb. It's best to provide them with cat towers to play on. If your cat enjoys being outdoors, ensure it is a safe environment where they won't run away or encounter predators. Cats are very intelligent and curious animals. They often like to scratch and claw at your furniture. A scratching post is a good solution to help prevent cats from scratching your items.

Friends:
Cats are usually social animals. However, some may be more outgoing than others; therefore, it's important to respect their needs. Many of them express affection and communicate with their owners through grooming and body language.

Did you know?
- - - - - - - - - - - - - - - -

• ancient Egyptians are believed to be the first group of people to domesticate cats
• on average, a cat sleeps between 12 and 16 hours per day
• a group of cats is called a clowder

- Chameleons -

Chameleons are known to be fragile and high-maintenance pets. They all have unique personalities and can change colors based on their health, temperature, and mood. There are over 200 species of chameleons; 76 of them can only be found in Madagascar.

Basic Needs

- chameleon enclosure
- food, water, and treats
- food and water bowl
- proper temperature, humidity, and lighting
- hiding spots, plants, and branches to climb
- substrate
- drip system

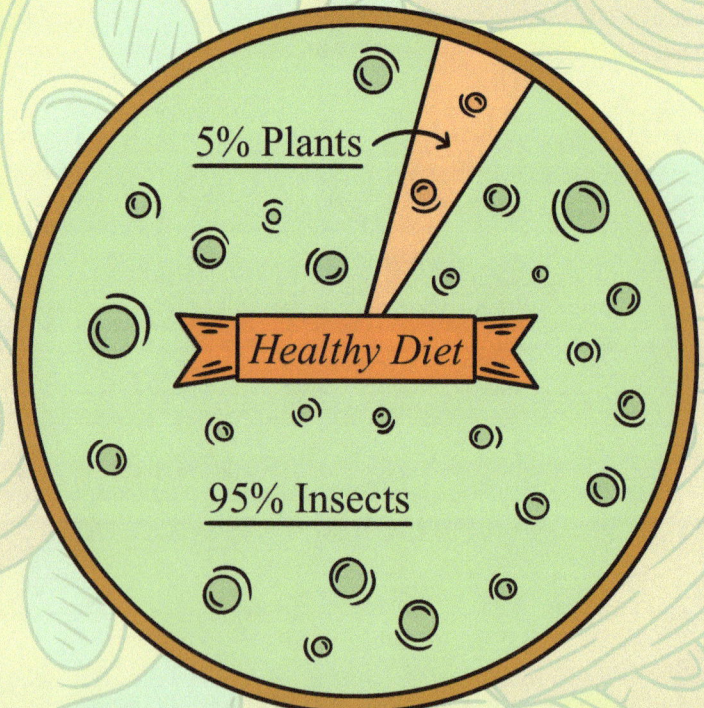

5% Plants

Healthy Diet

95% Insects

The perfect home for a chameleon will need to meet certain criteria. Their enclosure has to be tall, and the majority of their cage should be covered in branches and plants for them to climb on. Typically, chameleons get their water through droplets on leaves, so be sure to include a drip system in their enclosure to make sure they have the appropriate water intake. Chameleons will need exposure to light for about 12 hours a day. To help regulate your chameleon's body temperature, keep the bottom of their enclosure cool and around 70 to 75°F, while the top is warm and around 80 to 85°F.

Friends:
Chameleons tend to be solitary creatures that don't form social groups. They often live alone and only meet with others for mating purposes. You can bond with your pet chameleon by hand-feeding them or spending time near their enclosure.

Did you know?

• chameleons can live up to 10 years
• chameleons tongues are about twice as long as their body
• chameleons use their toes and tails to move and navigate the trees and bushes

- Chickens -

Chickens are commonly known to be farm animals, but many people still have them as pets. They are considered to be low-maintenance and beneficial because they lay eggs. There are not the most cuddly pets. However, some chickens are okay with being held.

Basic Needs

• chicken coop or shelter with roosting bars and nesting boxes
• food, water, and treats
• bedding such as straw, hemp, or pine shavings
• food and water bowl
• space to exercise
• dust baths

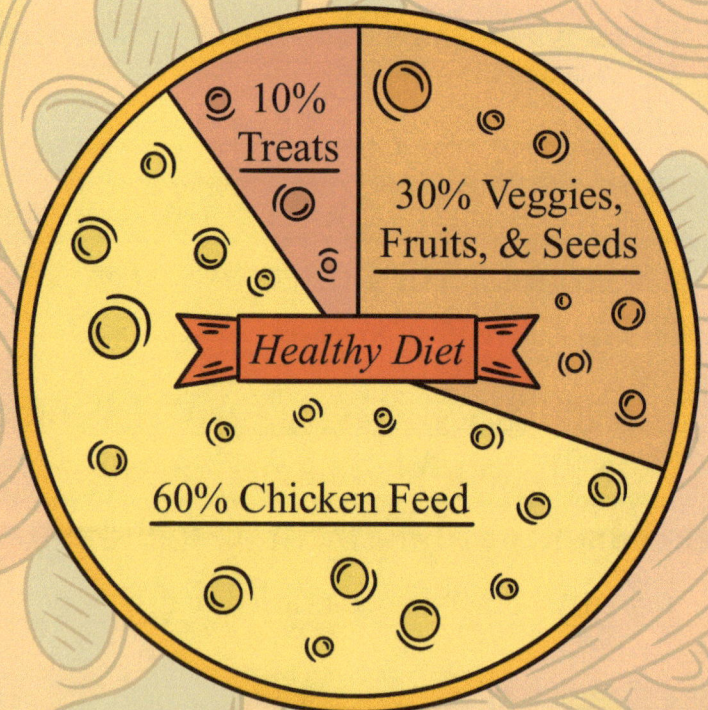

Healthy Diet

10% Treats

30% Veggies, Fruits, & Seeds

60% Chicken Feed

- Home -

Chickens thrive best in an environment where they have lots of space to roam and explore. It's important that they have an indoor space that protects them from predators. A chicken coop, barn, shed, and garage are suitable living spaces as long as they have everything they need with proper ventilation. Chickens should have access to a spacious outdoor area where they can dust bathe and forage. You should provide at least one nesting box for every 4 to 5 chickens. Depending on how deep the bedding layer is will determine how often you will need to clean the chickens home.

Friends:
Chickens are social animals that prefer to live with others rather than be alone. They often work together to find food, and chickens have a natural instinct to protect each other from predators by making sounds to alert the rest of the flock.

Did you know?

- chickens still have the ability to fly and can go short distances
- a chicken's earlobe can determine what color their eggshell is
- chickens have better color vision than humans do

- Chinchillas -

Chinchillas are usually quiet and considered to be low-maintenance pets. They have extremely soft fur and are primarily active at night. Chinchillas love to chew, so make sure they don't chew wires or plastic. Instead, provide safe toys or blocks made from wood.

Basic Needs

- chinchilla cage
- food, water, and treats
- a pair of nail clippers and a brush
- bedding material
- food and water bowl
- space to exercise
- chew toys
- dust baths

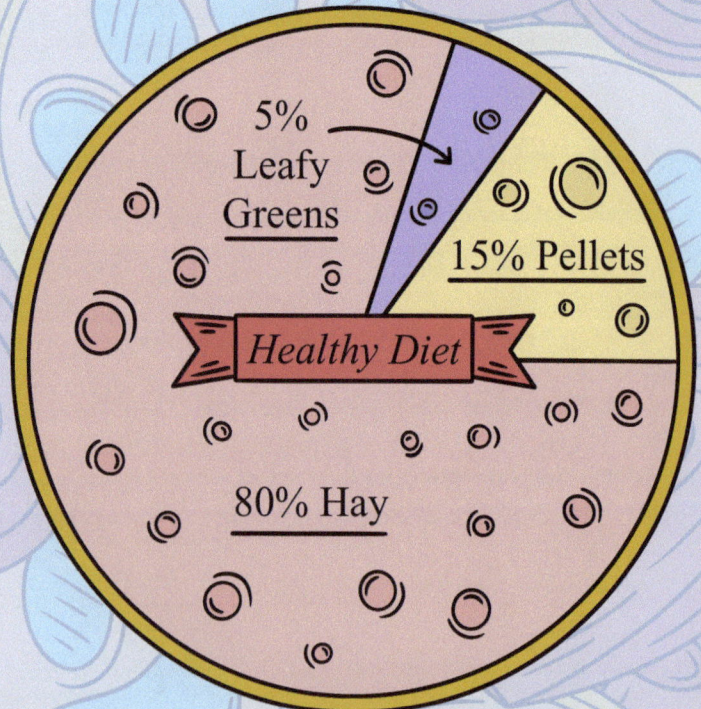

5%
Leafy
Greens

15% Pellets

Healthy Diet

80% Hay

- Home -

Chinchillas thrive in a home that provides them with lots of space and entertainment. It's best that they have an indoor enclosure that has lots of different platforms and levels to jump from. When choosing the cage, avoid picking any with wire bottom floors because it can cause foot injuries, and fill the bottom of the cage with bedding material such as aspen shavings. You will need to add a few nest boxes for your chinchillas to feel safe and secure. To maintain your chinchilla's fur and healthy skin, provide them with a container filled with specific chinchilla dust for them to roll in.

Friends:
Chinchillas are social animals and naturally live in social groups. It's important your pet chinchilla has a companion to groom, cuddle, and play with. A chinchilla without friends can lead to loneliness, boredom, and behavioral issues.

Did you know?
- - - - - - - - - - - - - - - -

• chinchillas are an endangered species
• chinchillas cannot stay in areas above 80°F because of their thick fur, making them prone to heatstrokes
• baby chinchillas are called kits

- Cows -

Cows are known as farm animals, but people still have them as pets. They are large animals that require lots of space. Cows are creatures of habit that thrive when they have a consistent daily routine. They have great memory as well as learning and problem-solving abilities.

Basic Needs

- shelter or barn
- food, water, and treats
- grooming products such as a brush and a curry comb
- food and water bowl
- regular hoof care
- pasture for cows to eat and exercise

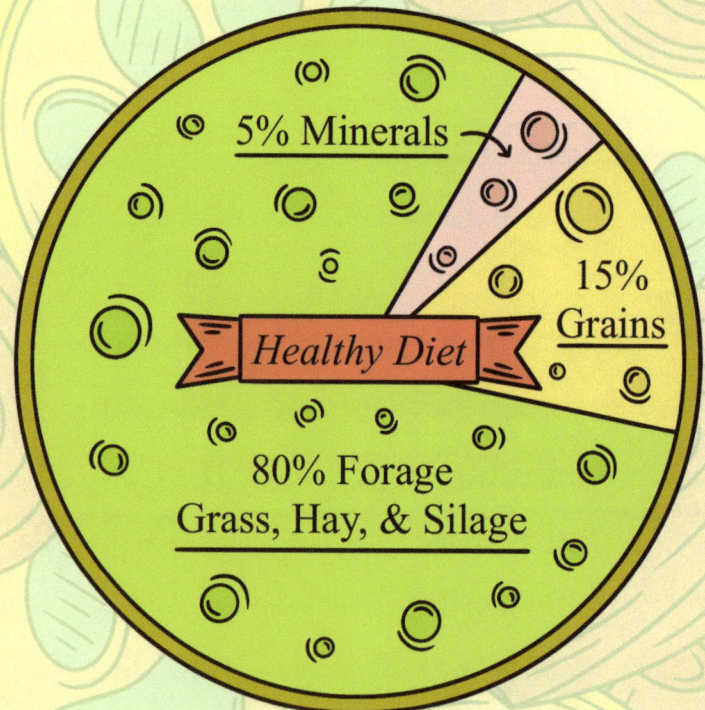

5% Minerals

15% Grains

Healthy Diet

80% Forage
Grass, Hay, & Silage

- Home -

The perfect home for a cow will need to meet a few specific requirements. Cows should have lots of space and room for them to move around freely and access a variety of nutritious grass. They must have an indoor living space, such as a barn, for them to rest in that will protect them from extreme weather, like intense heat. It's essential to have a sturdy fenced-in area for your cow to graze that prevents them from wandering off and finding themselves in dangerous situations. To support your cow's wellbeing, make sure you keep them in a peaceful and stress-free environment.

Friends:
Cows are social animals that enjoy the companionship of others. They get along well with animals, like horses and goats. Cows communicate with each other through mutual grooming, body language, and scent marking.

Did you know?

- cows are naturally good swimmers
- cows do not have upper front teeth and can chew at least 50 times a minute
- cows have the ability to sense odors up to 6 miles

- Dogs -

Dogs are among the most popular pets, and they make excellent companions. They can be loyal, friendly, and playful, as well as strong protectors and intelligent helpers. Dogs may learn more than 100 gestures and words. There are over 200 species of dogs.

Basic Needs

- dog bed
- food, water, and treats
- grooming products such as shampoo, nail clippers, and a brush
- food and water bowl
- collar and leash
- space to exercise
- chew toys

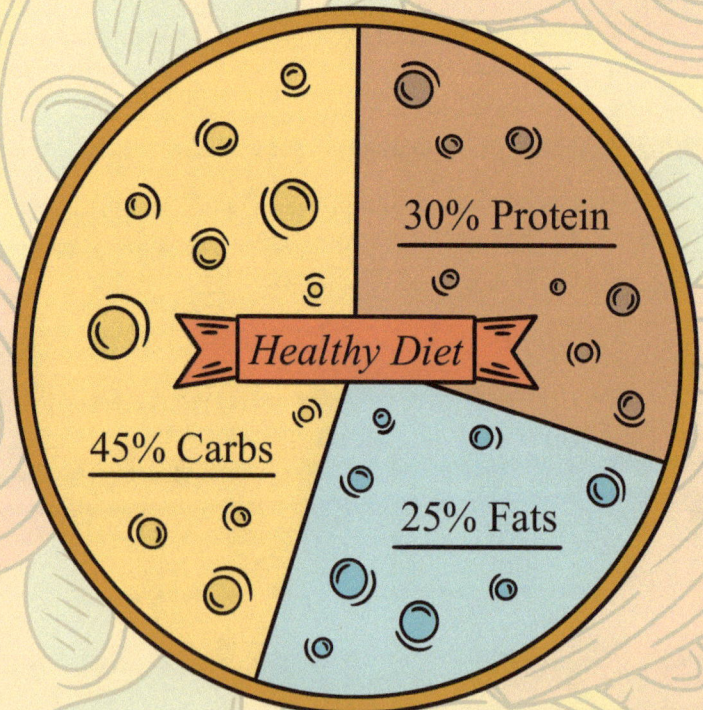

Healthy Diet

30% Protein

45% Carbs

25% Fats

- *Home* -

A dog's perfect home can depend on a number of factors, such as their breed, size, age, and personality. However, dogs perform best in an environment that provides them with lots of affection, care, exercise, mental stimulation, and a comfortable living space. Dogs require daily exercise, like walks or playtime. If you let them play in the yard, be sure it's safe and secure to protect them from predators and prevent them from running away. They constantly need mental stimulation to stop boredom and destructive behavior. You can give them toys and games to keep them entertained.

Friends:

Dogs are social animals that enjoy the company of others. You can bring your dog to dog parks to play and meet new friends. Some ways you can bond with your dog are through grooming, training, cuddling, and exercising together.

Did you know?
- - - - - - - - - - - - - - - - - -
• puppies are born deaf
• dogs' noses can sense thermal radiation
• dogs are among a small group of animals that show voluntary, unselfish kindness towards others without any reward

- Ducks -

Ducks are known to have sweet and friendly personalities. They make entertaining and loyal companions. There are over 120 species, and depending on which species you have, its life span will vary. However, on average, ducks live between 8 and 12 years.

Basic Needs

- duck coop or shelter that is predator-proof and well protected
- food, water, and treats
- place for them to swim and bathe
- food and water bowl
- space to exercise
- bedding

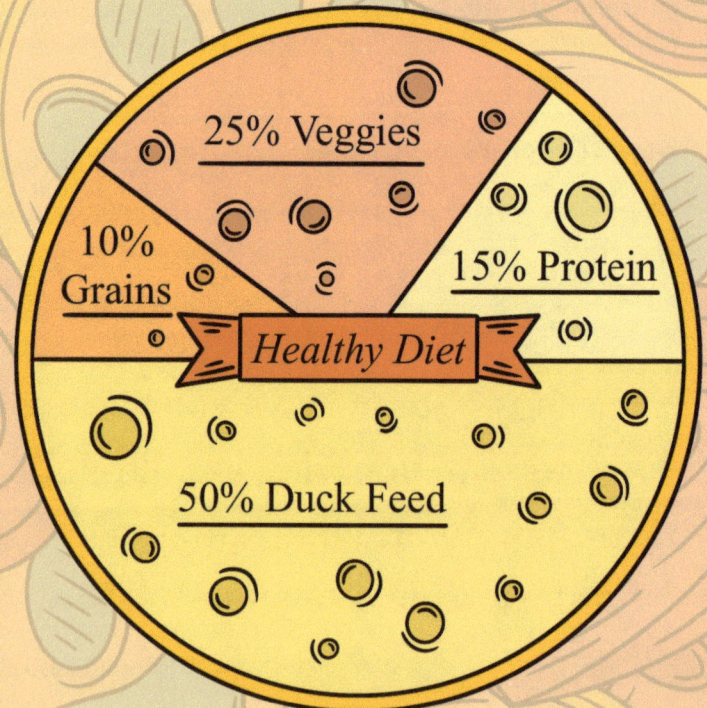

25% Veggies

10% Grains

15% Protein

Healthy Diet

50% Duck Feed

- Home -

The perfect home for ducks will need to meet a few requirements. Ducks need a safe and well-protected place for them to rest and feel secure in. They often move slowly, and most of them cannot fly, so it's important that the shelter you provide them is predator-proof. There should be at least four square feet of floor space per duck, and make sure proper ventilation is installed because ducks emit lots of moisture when they breathe, which can lead to mold or mildew growing inside their home. Ducks enjoy splashing and paddling around in water, so ensure they have access to a pond or kiddie pool.

Friends:
Ducks are very outgoing, and they get along extremely well with one another. They are most comfortable when they have companions and prefer living in groups rather than alone. You can bond with your ducks by hand-feeding them.

Did you know?

- ducklings can communicate with each other to coordinate hatchings
- ducks have the ability to dive 240 feet below the water
- ducks have waterproof feathers

- Ferrets -

Ferrets are known to be very playful, curious, and mischievous. They are also affectionate and can bring lots of entertainment and joy to a home. Ferrets can be trained to use the litter box and learn tricks. However, they also enjoy hiding things around the house.

Basic Needs

- spacious enclosure
- food, water, and treats
- soft bedding
- regular bathing and nail trimming
- food and water bowl
- space to exercise
- litter box
- hammock

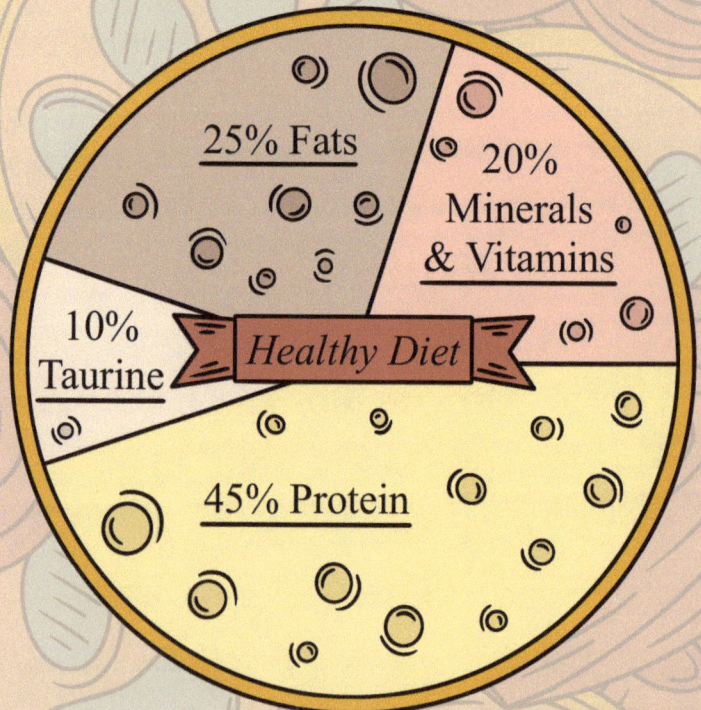

25% Fats

20% Minerals & Vitamins

10% Taurine

Healthy Diet

45% Protein

- Home -

The perfect home for ferrets will have lots of space to run and play. They are highly active creatures, so keeping them locked in a hutch all day will not be enough for them. There should be a designated space or room that is ferret-proof to allow them to release energy. Ferrets can be trained to use the litter box, so add one to their enclosure. Include soft bedding like blankets, and make sure all the flooring is solid and not wire mesh floors. Ferrets love to dig and sleep in hammocks, so be sure you include hammocks that fit more than one and a spot for them to dig in, like a box full of dry rice.

Friends:
Ferrets are social animals that thrive in groups. They enjoy playing with one another and exhibit behaviors like wrestling and chasing. Your pet ferret will seek companionship with other animals and humans, so make sure they are not kept alone.

Did you know?

• ferrets were one of the most popular pets during the 1990's
• the name ferret is derived from the Latin word "furittus," which means little thief
• a ferret's average lifespan is 8 years

- Fish -

Fish are extremely popular pets. They are low-maintenance and provide a calming and stress-relieving experience. Fish do not require the same level of attention or interaction as other pets do. However, they still bring lots of joy and beauty to a home.

Basic Needs

- fish tank with enough space for them to swim
- food and treats
- good-quality water
- appropriate lighting and temperature for the fish and aquatic plants
- decorations and hiding places

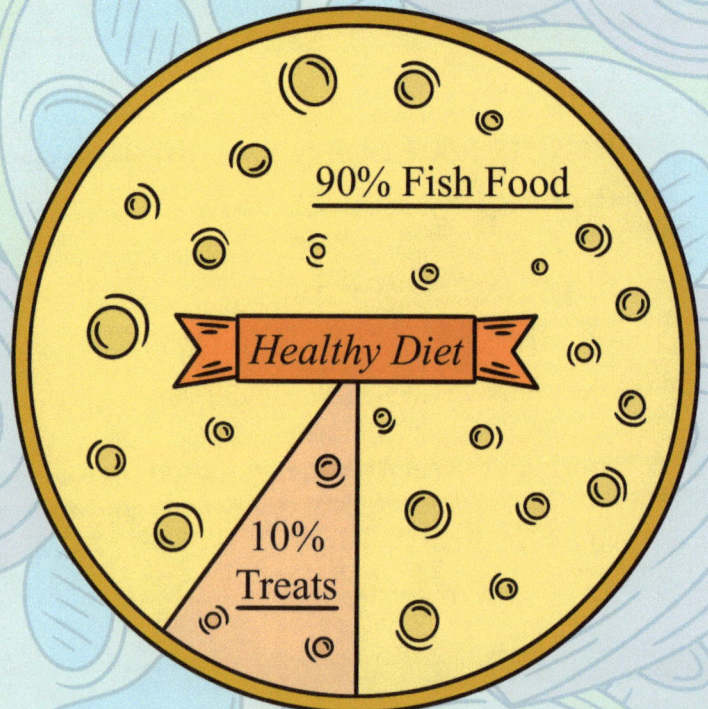

90% Fish Food

Healthy Diet

10% Treats

- *Home* -

A fish needs to be in an environment that has enough space for it to grow. There are many different types of fish, so be sure to do research on what type of fish you have and how big it will be to ensure you get the right size tank. A happy and healthy fish will be kept at a temperature of around 75°F. When finding a spot for your fish tank, avoid placing it in direct sunlight. You should clean your fish tank at least once a month to remove any bacteria. When decorating your fish tank, try to recreate a natural ocean-like environment, and be sure not to overcrowd it with too many items.

Friends:

Certain species of fish are very territorial and aggressive and do best living alone, while other species thrive on having others around and enjoy being in groups. When housing multiple fish, monitor their behaviors to see if they are compatible.

Did you know?

• certain fish have the ability to change colors
• most fish are unable to blink because they don't have eyelids
• fish are known to have great memories and can remember musical tunes

- Frogs -

Frogs make fascinating and low-maintenance companions. They are not as interactive as other pets. However, they enjoy hopping and swimming around. Frogs should not be handled regularly due to their sensitive skin. There are more than 7,000 species of frogs.

Basic Needs

- frog enclosure
- food, water, and treats
- food and water bowl
- substrate
- proper temperature, humidity, and lighting
- small pool for soaking
- logs, branches, and plants to climb

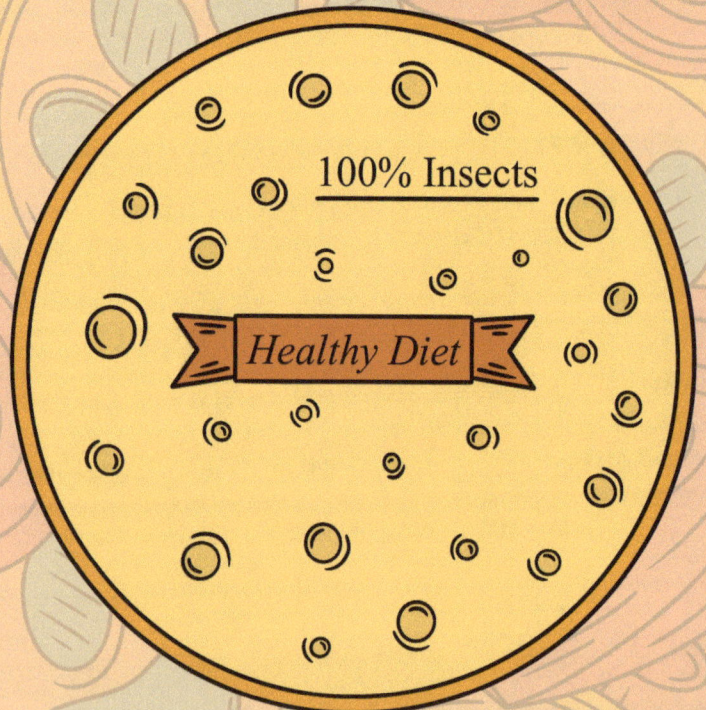

100% Insects

Healthy Diet

- *Home* -

A frog's perfect home will have to meet a few requirements. Frogs are amphibians, so they will need an enclosure that is half land and half water. The size of the tank, humidity levels, and temperature will depend on what species of frog you have. Keeping their enclosure clean is important because frogs tend to be very sensitive to waste and contaminants in their environment. A dirty enclosure can cause health issues like bacterial infections or fungal infections. You can include plants and branches in your frog's habitat, but avoid small rocks or gravel because they might accidentally ingest them.

Friends:
Frogs are mainly solitary creatures, and they don't engage in much social interaction. In order to bond with your frog, it's important that you give them attention and proper care. It's best if they see you as their source for food and comfort.

Did you know?

- the biggest frog in the world weighs more than 7 pounds
- some species of frogs can change color
- frogs can absorb water through their skin
- certain frogs have translucent skin

- Geckos -

Geckos are often considered low-maintenance pets. They are most active at night and love to climb and jump. Geckos are usually silent. However, occasionally they make noises like chirping, barking, and clicking. More than 1,600 species of geckos exist on Earth.

Basic Needs

- gecko enclosure
- food, water, and treats
- substrate
- food and water bowl
- appropriate lighting and temperature
- branches or driftwood to climb on
- space to exercise

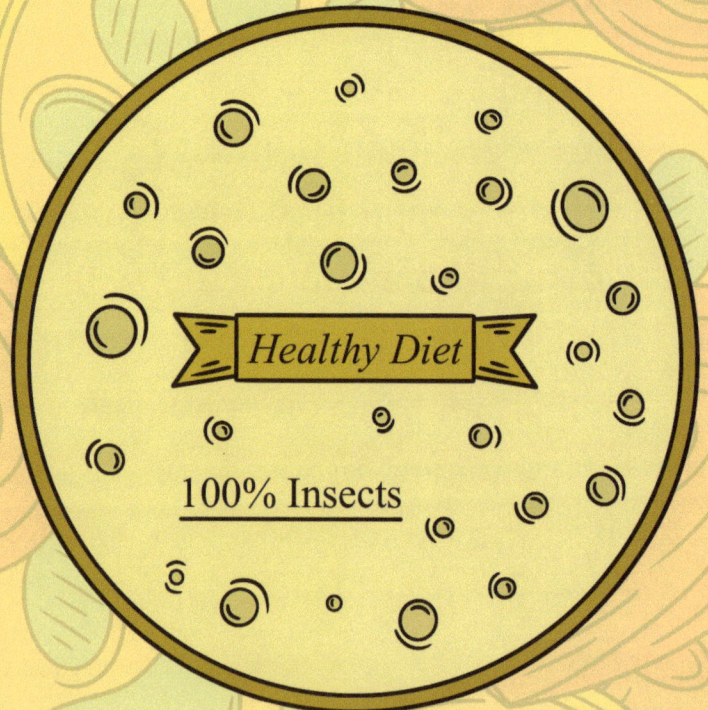

Healthy Diet

100% Insects

- Home -

Geckos thrive in an environment that allows them space to move around and exhibit their natural behaviors. A gecko enclosure is usually a 20-gallon aquarium. While picking out their enclosure, be sure it has a tight-fitting lid to prevent your gecko from escaping. The ideal temperature in your geckos home should be between 70 and 90°F. The humidity in their home should be kept between 70 and 90%. Additionally, you need to include lighting for a proper day and night cycle. To provide mental stimulation and enrichment for your gecko, add branches, plants, or rocks for them to hide in.

Friends:

Geckos are usually solitary animals that don't seek companionship from others. When handling your pet gecko, avoid grabbing their tail, as they often drop it as a natural defense. However, their tail always grows back.

Did you know?

- certain species of geckos have no legs and look like snakes
- geckos store fat and nutrients in their tails
- geckos can live for 10 to 20 years
- most geckos don't have eyelids

- Goats -

Goats are known to be extremely curious, playful, and intelligent. They have great problem solving skills and can easily adapt to their surroundings. Additionally, goats are commonly very affectionate pets. There are more than 300 species of goats in the world.

Basic Needs

- safe and secure shelter
- food, water, and treats
- grooming products like combs and brushes
- bedding for comfort
- food and water bowl
- pasture for goats to browse and exercise
- regular hoof care

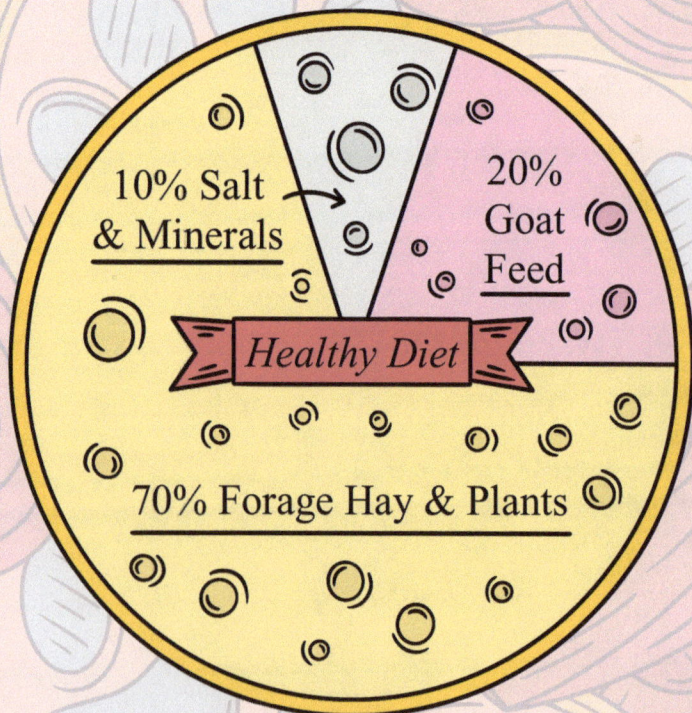

Healthy Diet

10% Salt & Minerals

20% Goat Feed

70% Forage Hay & Plants

Goats thrive in an environment that allows them space to explore and form healthy social dynamics. They require an indoor living space to protect them from predators and extreme weather. It's best to provide them with a pole barn that has proper ventilation and be sure to include bedding for the goats. Dirt for bedding is a popular option to provide comfort for your goats. However, dirt floors can be more difficult to clean and require regular maintenance. In addition, goats should have a safe, fenced-in outdoor space that allows them to forage, browse, and exercise.

Friends:

Goats are herd animals and always prefer living in groups. Being in a herd provides them with a sense of companionship and security. They are known to be quite vocal and typically form strong bonds with each other as well as with humans.

Did you know?

- baby goats are also known as kids
- goats sometimes sneeze to warn each other of danger
- goats can see about 320 to 340 degrees around them without having to move

- Guinea Pigs -

Guinea pigs have a very gentle and docile nature. They are less likely to bite or scratch, making them wonderful pets for families with young children. Guinea pigs enjoy communicating with others. They purr when they are feeling content and squeal when they are excited.

Basic Needs

- guinea pig cage
- food, water, and treats
- grooming products such as shampoo, nail clippers, and a brush
- food and water bowl
- bedding material
- space to exercise
- toys and tunnels

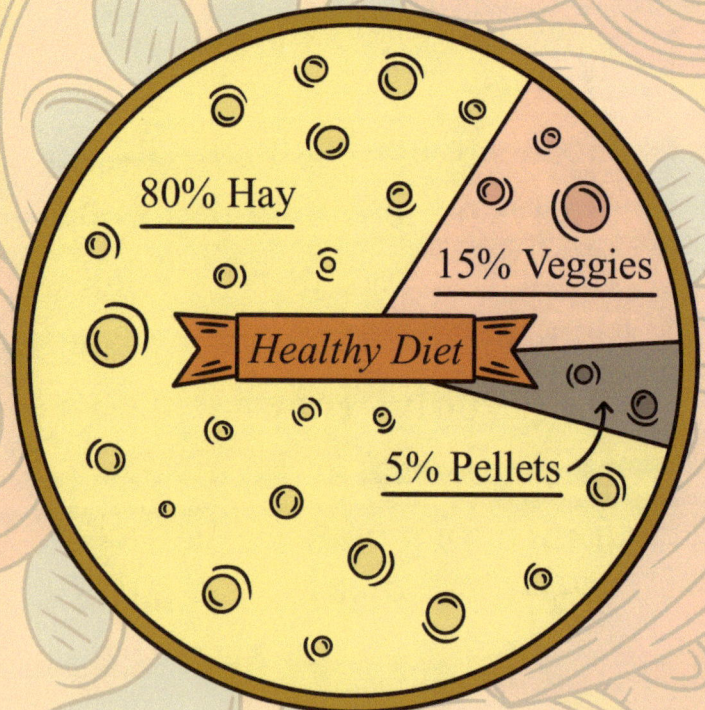

Healthy Diet

80% Hay

15% Veggies

5% Pellets

Guinea pigs thrive in a living space that is secure and large enough for them to move around, exercise, and stand up in. While picking out a cage, ensure that the bottom is completely solid with no holes to protect their feet and prevent injuries. When choosing the bedding for your guinea pig, avoid using cedar or pine shavings because they can be harmful for their respiratory system. It's best to use paper bedding and regularly clean the bedding to maintain an odor-free environment. Include multiple hideouts throughout the cage for your guinea pig to retreat and feel safe and comfortable.

Friends:
Guinea pigs enjoy interaction and companionship with humans as well as other guinea pigs. They love playing and chasing each other. Happy guinea pigs will popcorn, which are joyful jumps they do when they are extremely excited.

Did you know?
- - - - - - - - - - - - - - - - - -

• guinea pigs can live up to 14 years
• they don't sleep very long and are awake for almost 20 hours a day
• guinea pigs have more bones than humans
• guinea pigs are not related to pigs

- Hamsters -

Hamsters are considered to be low-maintenance and very entertaining pets. They enjoy running on wheels, exploring, and playing with their toys. Hamsters all have different personalities, and the majority of them like being petted. There are more than 20 species.

Basic Needs

- hamster cage with multiple hideouts
- food, water, and treats
- small nail clippers and a brush
- food and water bowl
- lots of toys
- exercise wheel
- bedding material

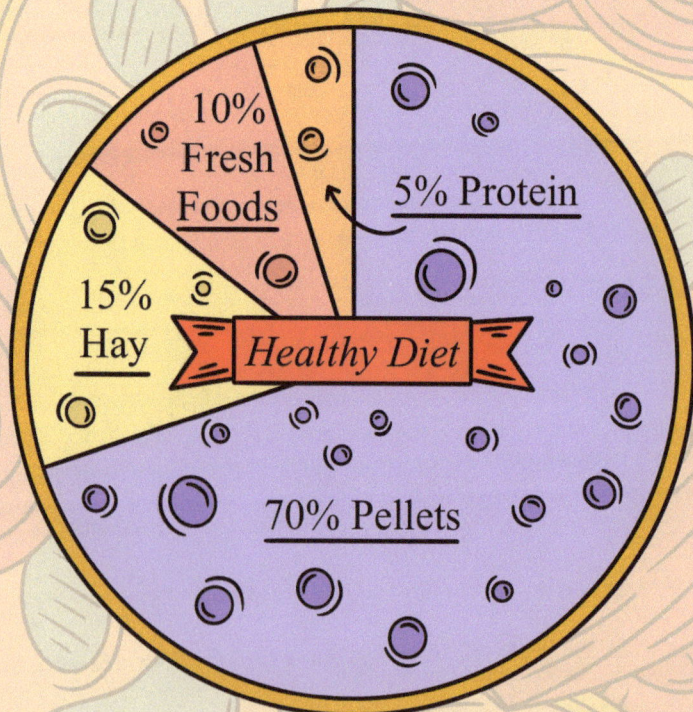

Healthy Diet

- 10% Fresh Foods
- 5% Protein
- 15% Hay
- 70% Pellets

- *Home* -

A hamster needs a spacious cage with lots of entertainment and toys to ensure their well-being and happiness. Their cage should be at least 12 inches tall and a minimum of 24 inches by 12 inches. However, the larger the cage, the better. A hamster wheel is an essential item for hamsters. It supports their physical and mental health while also preventing obesity. Hamsters are vulnerable to extreme temperatures, so it's best to keep them in a place that's room temperature. It is necessary for hamsters to have a natural light-dark cycle, so place them in a room that has natural sunlight.

Friends:

Hamsters are considered to be solitary animals and do not require the companionship of other hamsters because they can be quite territorial and aggressive toward one another. However, they still enjoy social interaction with people.

Did you know?

- hamsters do not have great eyesight and are colorblind
- hamsters have special pouches in their cheeks that can store food
- newborn hamsters are blind until there are two weeks old

- Hedgehogs -

Hedgehogs are usually shy and timid. While trying to hold them, you must be patient and establish trust with your hedgehog. If they feel threatened or scared, they will curl into a ball and raise their quills. Hedgehogs are active at night and enjoy playing with toys.

Basic Needs

- hedgehog cage
- food, water, and treats
- nail clippers
- bedding such as fleece
- food and water bowl
- space to exercise
- regular water baths
- toys, tunnels, and hiding spots

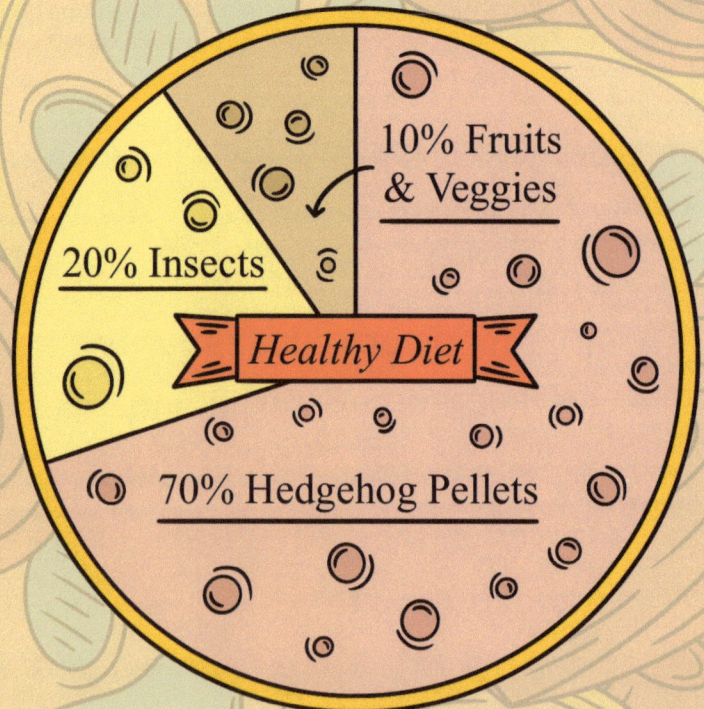

20% Insects

10% Fruits & Veggies

Healthy Diet

70% Hedgehog Pellets

- *Home* -

Hedgehogs thrive in an environment that allows them space to roam and explore. When choosing their cage, make sure it has a solid bottom rather than a wire bottom because their legs may become stuck or severely harmed. All hedgehog homes will need a type of bedding; some popular choices include fleece and recycled paper pellets. Avoid using cedar shavings, as they frequently irritate hedgehogs lungs. Your hedgehog will require some sort of entertainment as well as a place to hide and feel secure, so consider adding a large exercise wheel, cozy hideout pouches, and igloos.

Friends:
Hedgehogs are primarily solitary animals, and it's best if they are housed alone.
However, if having multiple hedgehogs living in the same space is something that interests you, females are more likely to get along than males.

Did you know?

- hedgehogs have around 7,000 spikes on their back
- hedgehogs can travel up to 2 miles
- groups of hedgehogs are called prickles
- hedgehogs can run about 5 mph

- Horses -

Horses make lovely companions for those with the commitment, space, and resources to provide proper care. Having a pet horse can be quite expensive, and it's very important that you learn how to handle and ride horses for your own and the horse's safety.

Basic Needs

- horse stable
- food, water, and treats
- grooming products such as a brush and a curry comb
- food and water bowl
- regular hoof care
- pasture for horses to eat and exercise

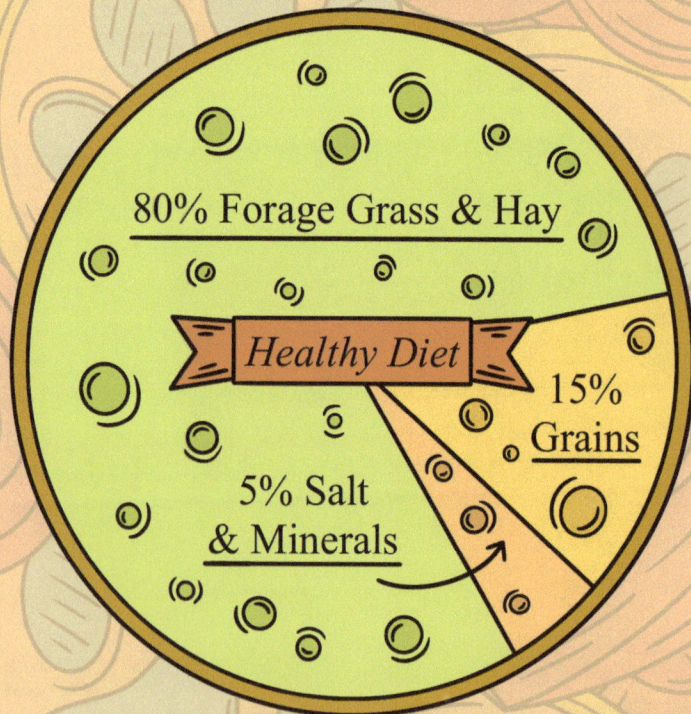

80% Forage Grass & Hay

Healthy Diet

15% Grains

5% Salt & Minerals

- Home -

The perfect environment for horses includes plenty of space for them to exercise; it's best that they can roam free in a large pasture so they can graze and explore. The pasture makes up the majority of the horse's diet, so it's crucial to maintain a healthy pasture and monitor for any poisonous plants growing to prevent health issues. Horses must have a well-ventilated and sturdy shelter to protect them from harsh weather conditions such as snow, rain, or extreme heat. Be sure that your horse's environment is safe and secure from potential predators or objects that may cause injuries.

Friends:
Horses are social animals that do best when they have companionship. Horses rely on one another for communication, protection, and mutual support. If horses are isolated or deprived of socialization, they can start developing behavioral issues.

Did you know?

- - - - - - - - - - - - - - - - - -

• horses can live for over 30 years
• it takes about 9 to 12 months for an entire horse hoof to regrow
• horses can produce approximately 10 gallons of saliva per day

- Llamas -

Llamas are considered to be high-maintenance pets and are known to have a very calm and gentle demeanor. They are intelligent and have great senses of sight and hearing. This allows them to adapt to their surroundings and alerts them to potential threats nearby.

Basic Needs

• barn with bedding
• food, water, and treats
• grooming products such as a brush and a pair of shears
• food and water bowl
• pasture for llamas to graze and exercise
• regular hoof care

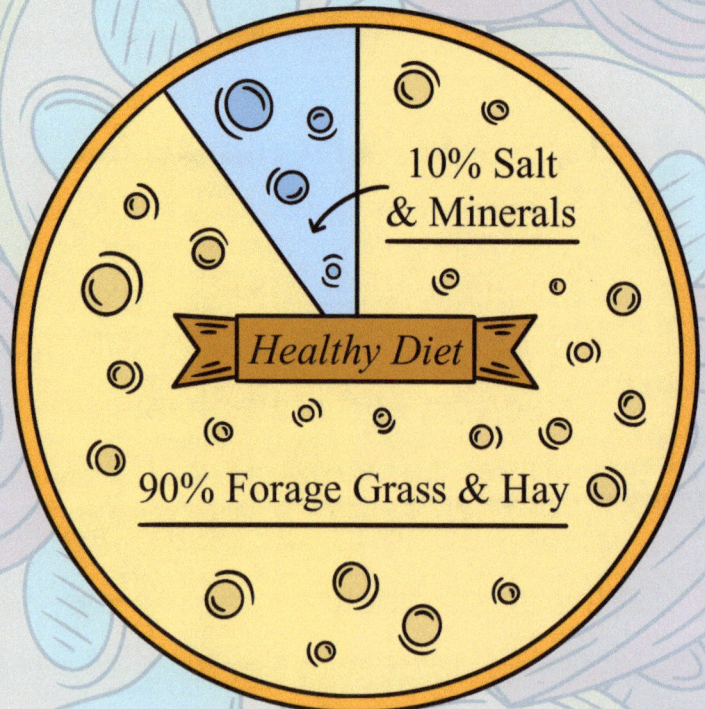

Healthy Diet

10% Salt & Minerals

90% Forage Grass & Hay

- *Home* -

When creating your llamas perfect home, pole barns are one of the best shelters to keep your llamas safe and protected. There will need to be bedding for the llamas to rest on and stay warm in during the winter. You can use clean straw or wood shavings for bedding, and it's important to always replace them whenever they're soiled to prevent serious health risks from occurring. Llamas require a fenced-in outdoor space where they can explore and graze. Provide at least 2,000 square feet of grazing area per llama, and make sure the outdoor area is free from any toxic plants that can harm them.

Friends:
Llamas prefer to live in groups rather than alone, and they naturally form herds for companionship and protection. To bond with your llama, approach them calmly and offer treats to build a positive association with your presence.

Did you know?

- - - - - - - - - - - - - - - - -

• llamas spit can be flung more than 10 feet
• llamas stick their tongues out at each other to express anger
• llamas are native to South America
• llamas usually live up to 20 years

- Mice -

Mice are low-maintenance and quiet pets. They are nocturnal animals, which means they are most active at night. A well-cared-for mouse can live between 1 and 3 years. Mice are known for their friendly and curious nature. There are more than 1,000 species.

Basic Needs

- cozy home
- food, water, and treats
- grooming products such as nail clippers and a brush
- food and water bowl
- bedding
- space to exercise
- chew toys

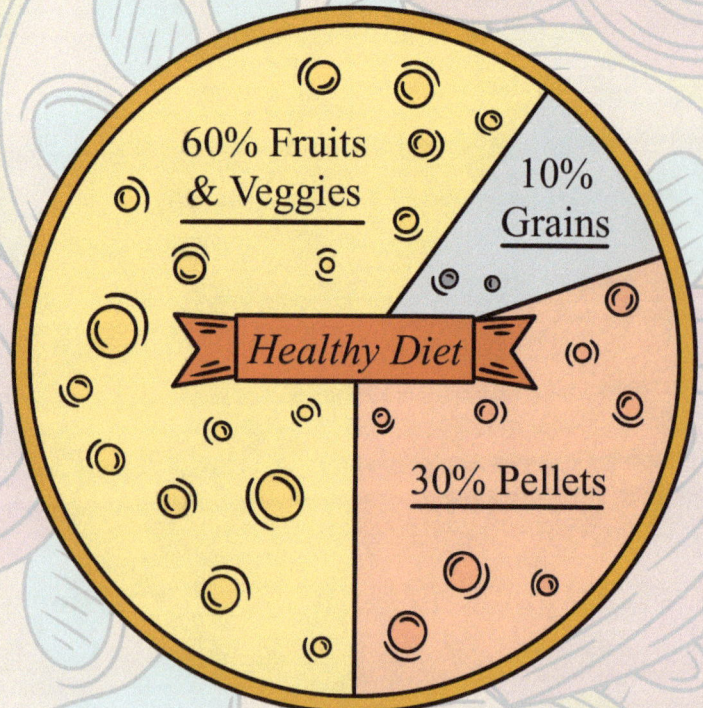

Healthy Diet

60% Fruits & Veggies

10% Grains

30% Pellets

- Home -

The ideal home for mice will need to meet certain requirements. It's best to have as large of an enclosure as possible to allow them plenty of space to exercise. When choosing your bedding, avoid using any kind of material that creates dust because mice are more susceptible to developing breathing problems. The location of their cage should be indoors, out of direct sunlight, and kept away from loud noises or lots of vibrations. While picking fun activities for your mice, be sure to get them lots of toys and different objects for them to climb up and down on, such as tunnels, ropes, or ladders.

Friends:
Mice enjoy engaging and interacting with their friends. They communicate with each other to coordinate group activities. If mice are kept isolated for extended periods of time, they can start showing signs of loneliness or boredom.

Did you know?

- mice have a strong sense of smell, and they don't like cheeses that produce a strong odor
- mice snack between 15 and 20 times a day
- mice are fantastic jumpers, climbers, and swimmers

- Parrots -

Parrots are highly intelligent pets known for their problem-solving skills, learning ability, and humor. They are affectionate and imitate human speech, sounds, and music. Parrots are emotionally sensitive and have a very playful nature. There are more than 300 species.

Basic Needs

- large parrot cage
- food, water, and treats
- grooming products such as a bathing dish and nail clippers
- food and water bowl
- wood perches
- space to exercise
- lots of toys

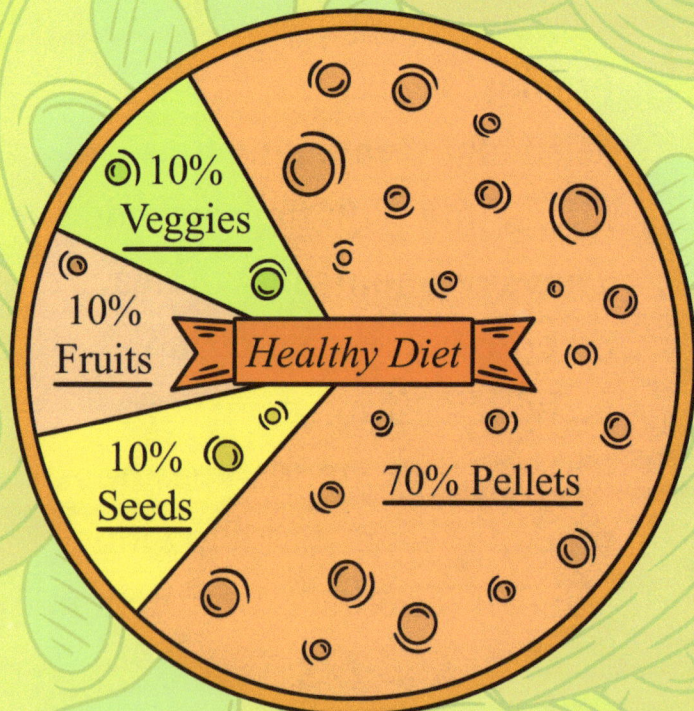

Healthy Diet

10% Veggies

10% Fruits

10% Seeds

70% Pellets

- *Home* -

A parrot's perfect home should meet several crucial requirements. Their cage must be spacious enough for them to stretch their wings and move around comfortably, as well as have enough room for toys, accessories, and perches. When picking a cage for your parrot, it's best to find the largest possible cage within your available space. It is also important to pick a cage with the appropriate bar spacing that prevents them from getting their head, feet, or beak caught between the bars. Be sure you spend time with your parrot and allow it opportunities to exercise outside of their cage.

Friends:
Parrots are very social animals. They can develop extremely strong bonds with people. The bond between you and your parrot can be strengthened by regular social interaction, such as talking, playing games, or playing with toys.

Did you know?
- - - - - - - - - - - - - - - - - -
• parrots are one of the only animals able to imitate human speech
• parrots can live over 100 years
• certain species of parrots are said to be the most intelligent animals on Earth

- Pigs -

Pigs are able to make fantastic companions. They vary in size and can weigh between 50 and 200 pounds. Pigs are very intelligent animals and have the ability to learn tricks, understand commands, and use the litter box. Contrary to many beliefs, pigs are quite clean.

Basic Needs

- pig shelter
- food, water, and treats
- grooming products like soap and brushes
- food and water bowl
- bedding, such as straw or wood shavings
- space to exercise
- pig toys

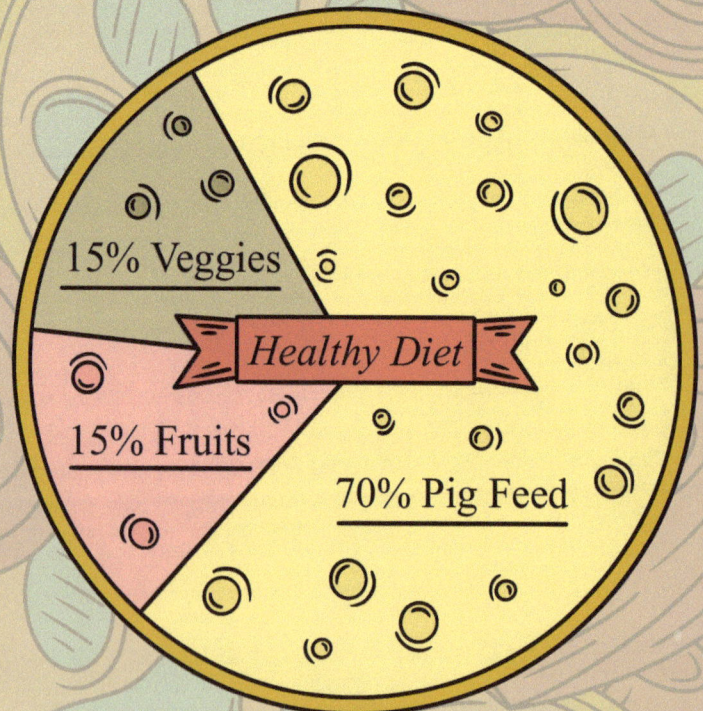

Healthy Diet

15% Veggies

15% Fruits

70% Pig Feed

- Home -

A pig's perfect home will consist of lots of outdoor as well as indoor space for them to explore and exercise in. While creating a living space for your pig, always prioritize their foot safety. Pigs are highly susceptible to foot issues, and if this goes unnoticed, it can be extremely expensive to treat. To avoid this problem, keep them away from slippery surfaces and limit their time on hard surfaces like concrete. It's best to keep the pigs dry with clean straw. Pigs love and need mud. Mud helps them keep cool and acts as a natural sunscreen to protect their skin. In addition, mud keeps insects away.

Friends:
Pigs are very social animals. They like living in groups and can form strong relationships with both humans and other pigs. They play with one another, and some activities they enjoy are wrestling, chasing, and exploring.

Did you know?

- pigs do not have the ability to sweat
- March 1st is National Pig Day
- baby pigs are called piglets, and mother pigs are called sow
- pigs can live up to 20 years

- Rabbits -

Rabbits are high-maintenance and sensitive pets that are fragile and easily frightened. However, they make wonderful companions. Rabbits need space to hop around and do binkies, which is a twist and jump in the air that occurs when they're full of happy energy.

Basic Needs

- rabbit hutch or hideout
- food, water, and treats
- a brush, scissors, and nail clippers
- food and water bowl
- liter box filled with pine pellets and hay
- space to exercise
- rabbit chew toys

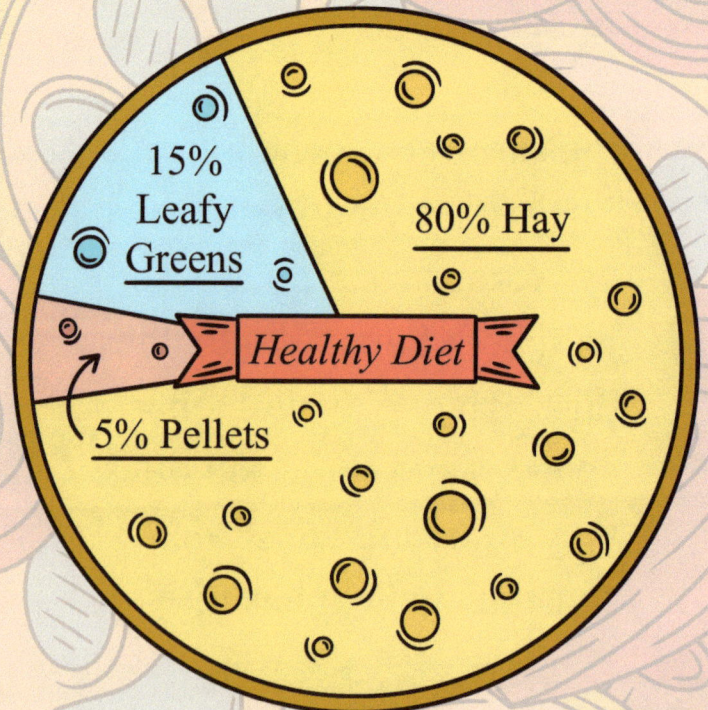

Healthy Diet

- 80% Hay
- 15% Leafy Greens
- 5% Pellets

- *Home* -

A rabbit's perfect home is safe, comfortable, and cozy, with enough space for them to hop around and exercise. If your rabbits live outdoors, make sure they can't escape by jumping, digging, or encountering dangerous predators. If your rabbits live indoors, make sure all your wires are covered or hidden because they like to chew. It's important that, no matter where they live, they have a hideout and room to exercise. Rabbits can be liter-box trained and are self-grooming animals. It's crucial to know not to give rabbits a bath due to their natural oils that keep their fur and skin healthy.

Friends:
Rabbits are social animals, and they always do better in pairs. It's best to have two rabbits instead of one because it prevents loneliness and boredom. Having a pair of bonded rabbits will also keep each other calmer and happier.

Did you know?
- - - - - - - - - - - - - - - - - - -
• rabbits teeth never stop growing; chewing hay prevents them from being overgrown
• rabbits are the third most common animal found at shelters
• sometimes rabbits eat their own poop

- Scorpions -

Scorpions are low-maintenance and make fascinating pets. They use their pinchers and stingers to catch prey. Generally, scorpions are not common pets and are considered to be among the group of exotic pets. There are around 2,000 species of scorpions.

Basic Needs

• aquarium tank
• food, water, and treats
• bedding such as sand, coco fiber, or peat moss
• food and water bowl
• proper temperature, humidity, and lighting
• hiding spots like rocks and bark

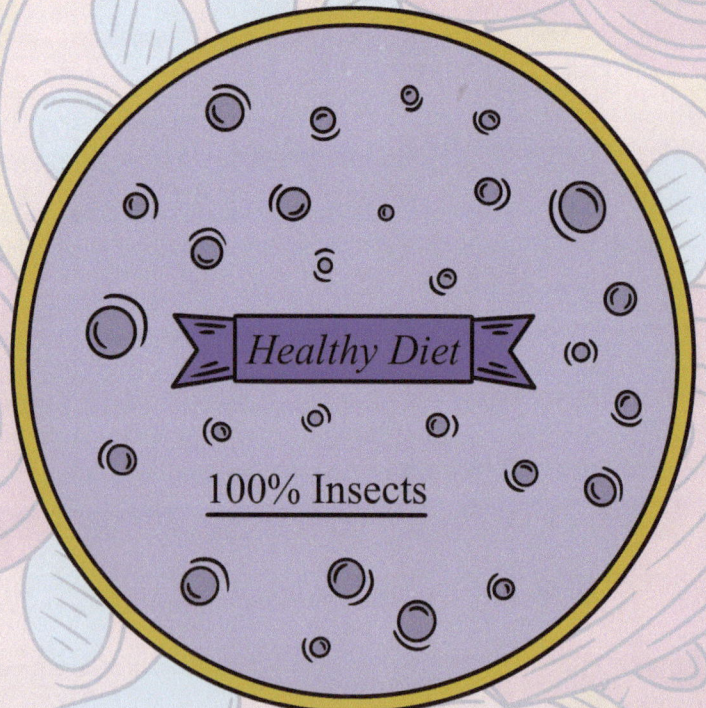

Healthy Diet

100% Insects

- Home -

In general, scorpions thrive in an environment that's got the proper amount of moisture, space, and places to hide, such as wood or pieces of a ceramic plant pot. A scorpion needs a secure enclosure that will maintain an appropriate humidity level and temperature. A good option is a glass aquarium with an escape-proof or lockable lid. Your choice of substrate will depend on whether you have a forest or desert species of scorpion. If you have a forest species, you can include peat moss and cover it with orchid bark chippings. If you have a desert species, it's best to add sand to their enclosure.

Friends:
Scorpions are primarily solitary creatures and they typically don't form social bonds with other other. They're known to be aggressive and territorial. Scorpions tend to engage in combat rather than have a cooperative interaction.

Did you know?

- - - - - - - - - - - - - - - -

• scorpions glow in UV lighting
• some scorpions can go for as long as 12 months without eating
• around 25 species of scorpions possess a toxin that is capable of killing humans

- Sheep -

Sheep are moderately high-maintenance pets. In general, sheep are known for being calm and peaceful; it is uncommon for a sheep to be hostile. They are exceptionally intelligent animals that can be trained to follow commands and perform tricks.

Basic Needs

- shelter or barn
- food, water, and treats
- grooming products such as a brush and a pair of shears
- food and water bowl
- pasture for sheep to graze and exercise
- regular hoof care

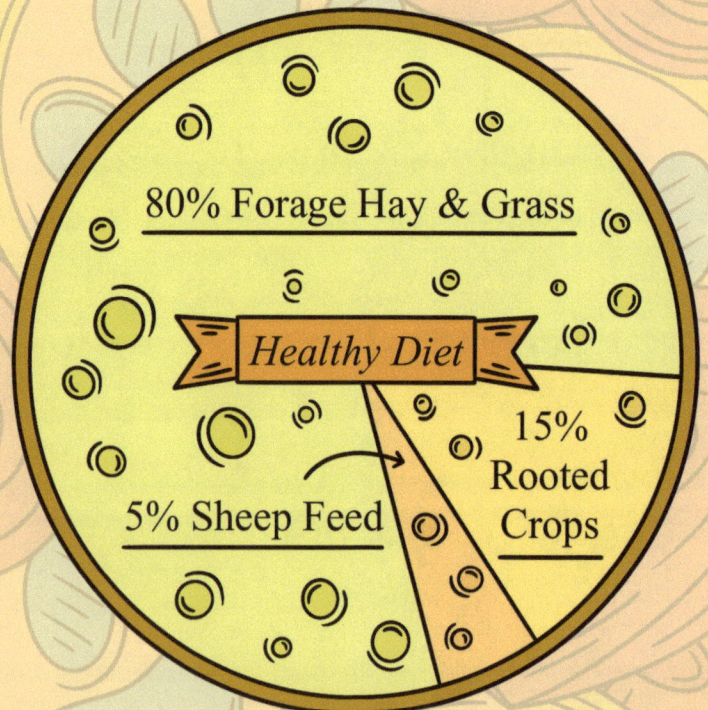

Healthy Diet

80% Forage Hay & Grass

15% Rooted Crops

5% Sheep Feed

Sheep thrive in an environment with lots of space for them to roam and exercise. They require an indoor living space to provide them comfort and protection from the weather and predators. Sheep should have access to a pasture where they can graze on grass. When choosing the bedding for your sheep, you have a variety of options. Hay is commonly used and will keep sheep warm during the colder months. Pine shavings are another bedding type used for their absorbency. However, this type of material clings on to the sheep's coat, making it more difficult to cut their hair.

Friends:
Sheep are social animals that prefer to live in groups. They naturally form flocks, and this provides them with a sense of security and safety. Sheep seek companionship during times of stress or loneliness, so make sure your sheep has a friend.

Did you know?

• sheep self-medicate when they feel ill by instinctively choosing to eat specific plants to make themselves feel better
• sheep can produce 2 to 30 pounds of wool a year

- Snails -

Snails are very low-maintenance pets that don't shed, smell, or make lots of noise. They are known to be most active at night and in damp environments. Depending on the species, some snails can live for a few years, while others can live for several decades with proper care.

Basic Needs

- snail enclosure
- food, water, and treats
- substrate made from peat moss or coco fiber
- food and water bowl
- appropriate humidity level and temperature
- places to hide like rocks or bark

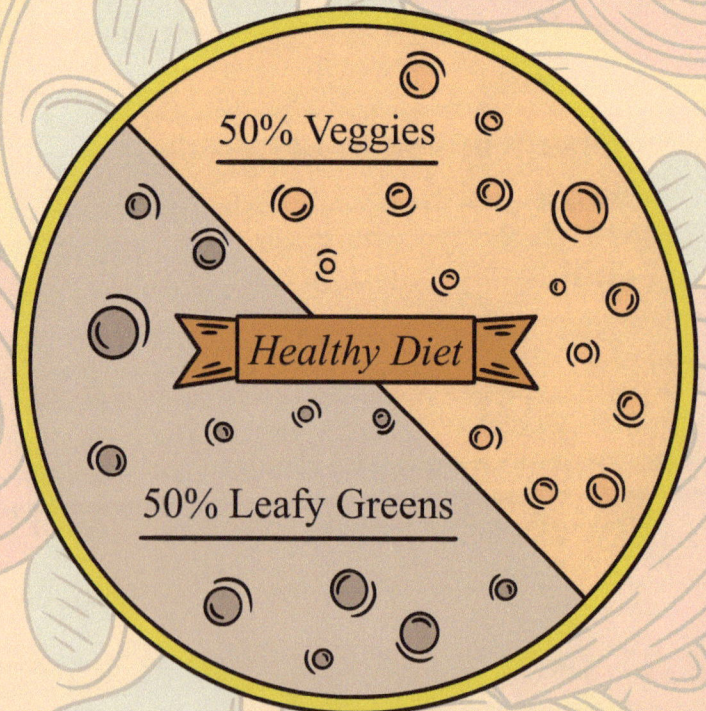

50% Veggies

Healthy Diet

50% Leafy Greens

- Home -

Snails thrive in a home that imitates their natural environment. They will need a large plastic or glass terrarium to live in. Ideally, it should be a 1-gallon tank per snail; if you're housing multiple snails, always go with a larger size. When adding substrate to your snail's home, you can use sterilized soil made for pets. Avoid using soil from your garden because it most likely contains parasites. You can add real plants to their home, but be sure they are not toxic to snails. Snails love to climb, so place some bark, sticks, leaves, and rocks inside their home for them to explore and be entertained.

Friends:
Snails do not interact the same way traditional pets do. However, hand feeding is a way you can bond with your snail. When holding your snail, it's important that you're gentle and handle them with care because they are extremely fragile.

Did you know?

- as snails grow, their shell grows with them
- some species of snails have more than 14,000 teeth that are located on their tongue
- some snails have both female and male reproductive organs

- Snakes -

Snakes make great pets and are clean, quiet, and usually odorless. There are many different species and types of snakes. Some may be more aggressive than others. However, in general, captive-bred snakes tend to be calmer, more relaxed, and easier to handle.

Basic Needs

- snake enclosure
- food, water, and treats
- appropriate humidity and temperature
- snake bedding
- food and water bowl
- space to exercise
- branches and places to hide

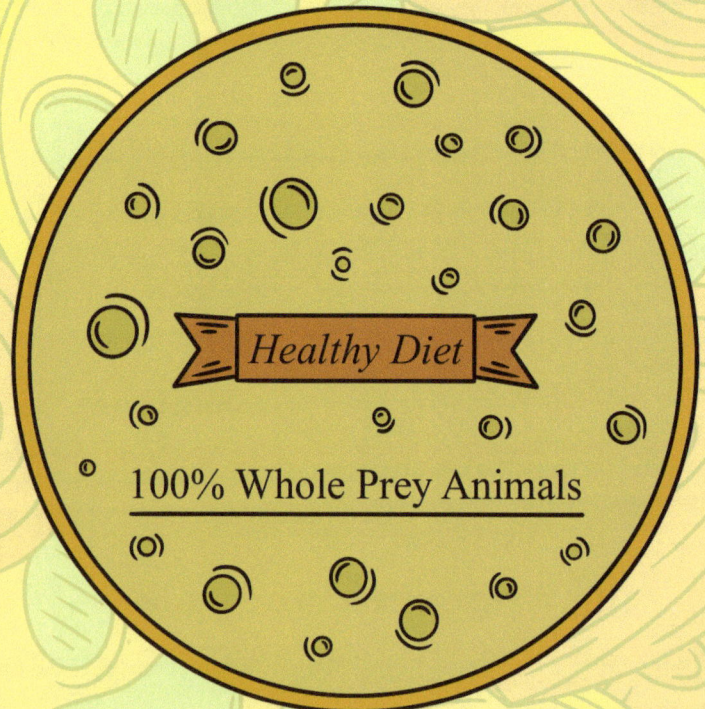

Healthy Diet

100% Whole Prey Animals

- Home -

A snake's perfect home can depend on several factors, like its type and size. When choosing an enclosure for your snake, avoid any with wire because snakes may strike or rub against it, causing damage to their face and skin. Stick to choosing enclosures designed for reptiles or pet snakes, like a terrarium. It's important that your snake has space to stretch and move around freely. Snakes are escape artists and can squeeze through small openings and push open covers, so make sure your enclosure is secure. Be sure to create an environment that mimics the snake's natural habitat.

Friends:
Snakes prefer to live alone, and they don't often form bonds or engage with other snakes. They can be very territorial and may show aggression toward others. However, some species of snakes may be okay with living in pairs or small groups.

Did you know?

- snakes smell with their tongues
- some species of snakes have the ability to glide through the air
- snakes eat anything that fits in their mouth
- snakes can hear through vibrations

- Tarantulas -

Tarantulas are known as quiet and low-maintenance pets. They aren't very active and are slow movers. There are more than 900 species, so depending on which species you have, it will determine if they are calm or aggressive. Tarantulas are delicate and can be easily injured.

Basic Needs

- tarantula housing
- food, water, and treats
- substrate made from peat moss or coco fiber
- food and water bowl
- space to exercise
- appropriate humidity and temperature
- hiding places

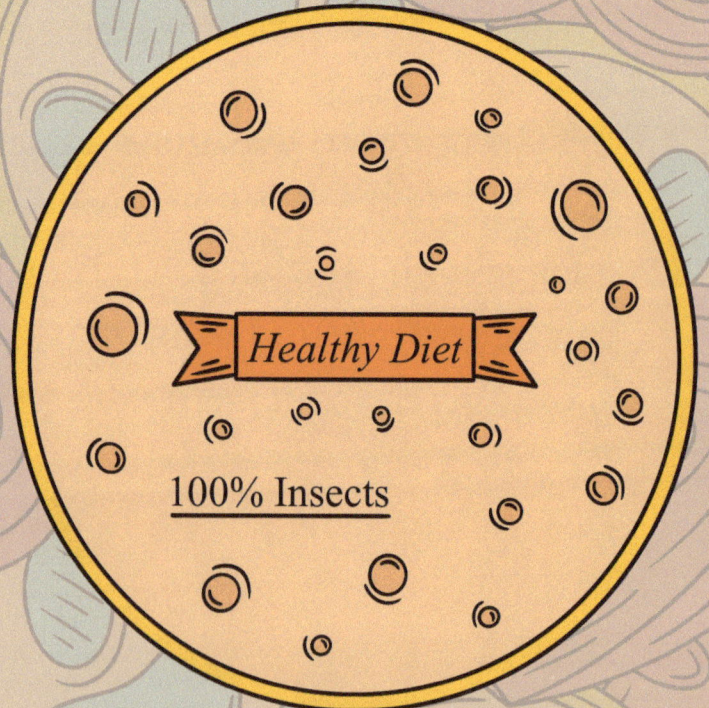

Healthy Diet

100% Insects

- Home -

Tarantulas thrive best in an environment that allows them to move around comfortably. When choosing your pet tarantula's enclosure, it's good to choose one that's at least three times the length of your tarantula. Be sure that your enclosure has proper ventilation, such as a mesh lid, to allow fresh air to circulate. While adding the substrate to the enclosure, make sure it is deep enough for the tarantula to burrow in. Tarantulas love hiding spots. You can add artificial caves, hollow logs, and cork bark to help your tarantula feel safe and secure. This will also help reduce its stress.

Friends:
Tarantulas prefer to live alone rather than in groups. They are known to be territorial and like to defend their space if they feel threatened. By keeping multiple tarantulas in the same enclosure, it may lead to stress-related health issues, injuries, or death.

Did you know?

• some species of tarantulas can live for 30 years
• female tarantulas live longer than male ones
• they can flick bristles at predators
• tarantulas have 8 eyes

- Turtles -

Turtles require more maintenance than many people think. They aren't the most affectionate and social pets. Many of them will become stressed if they are often held or touched. However, some may tolerate gentle handling. There are more than 300 species.

Basic Needs

- a turtle enclosure that has both a dry area and a water area
- food, water, and treats
- aquarium filter to keep the water clean
- food and water bowl
- appropriate lights and temperature

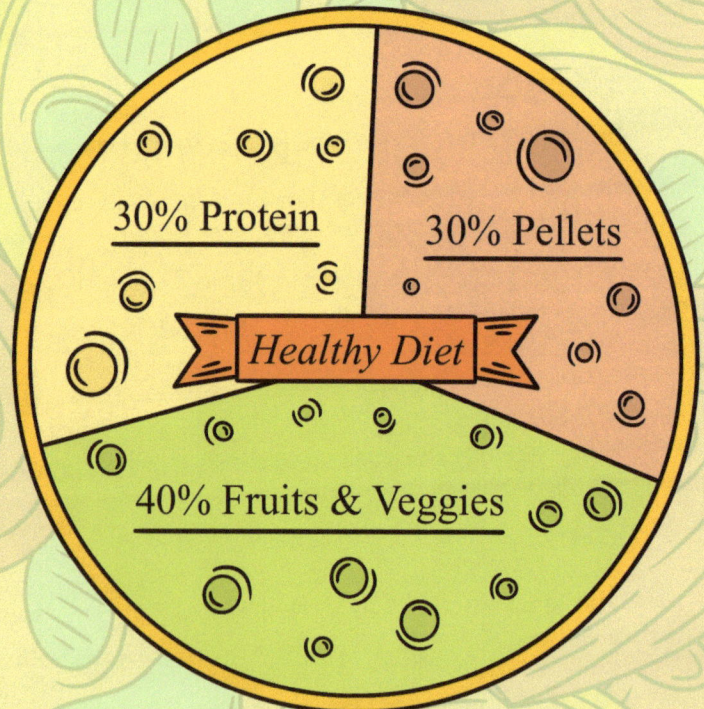

30% Protein

30% Pellets

Healthy Diet

40% Fruits & Veggies

- *Home* -

The perfect environment for a turtle should accommodate its size and allow it to grow. Glass and acrylic aquariums are popular choices for a pet turtle's home. When keeping your turtle indoors, be sure you set up a proper filtration system as well as lighting to ensure your turtle is comfortable and safe. If you have the space and the right climate, your pet turtle can live in outdoor ponds. When living outdoors, there must be a secure fence as well as a cover to protect them from predators. Whichever housing option you choose, it's important to regularly monitor their water quality.

Friends:
Turtles are not considered to be social animals. However, each species shows different behaviors. Some species may be more friendly, while others like to be alone. Certain turtles can also be more aggressive and territorial toward others.

Did you know?

- baby turtles are called hatchlings
- turtles can hold their breath underwater for approximately 5 hours
- the gender of some turtle species can be influenced by the temperature

- Lost Pets -

Unfortunately, it is very common for pets to run away or go missing. Some of these pets return home, while others are lost forever. This is an issue that occurs in many households. However, there are precautions you can take to prevent this from happening to your pet.

Precautions

- microchip your pet
- secure your yard, living space, and pet enclosure
- make sure to close all doors to ensure your pet doesn't sneak out
- place a proper collar on your pet

It is estimated that 1 in 3 pets go missing in their lifetime.

- Missing -

If your pet is missing, search the immediate area. Start by looking in your home to see if they are hiding or trapped somewhere. Then look in your yard and the areas surrounding your house. It is common for pets to hide in nearby bushes. If your pet is still not found, reach out to local animal shelters, veterinary clinics, and animal control agencies. Provide them with your contact information and your pet's photo and description in case they are brought in. Lastly, you can spread awareness through online platforms, create flyers, and offer a reward if your pet is found.

Stay Positive:
It's very important to not give up if your pet is missing. Some pets are found days, weeks, months, or years after they went missing. However, all of this can be prevented if you keep an eye on your pet and properly train them.

Did you know?

• July 4th is one of the most common days of the year for pets to go missing
• approximately 10 million pets go missing every year, and about 80% of them are never found

- Responsibility -

Being responsible before getting a pet is very important. Pets require time, effort, commitment, and attention. Pets are not disposable, and they become part of the family. It is inhumane to abandon your pet because you find it too challenging or less cute as they grow older.

Pet Owners

• need to understand that a pet requires your care for its entire life
• know the proper care and prioritize the safety, health, and wellbeing of your pet
• spend time and love your pet

Around 7 million pets enter the United States animal shelters every year, and about 2 million of them are euthanized.

- Are you ready for a pet? -

When deciding if you're ready for a pet, you must ask yourself if you are able to dedicate and commit your time, energy, love, and money to the animal for its entire life. Pets can be expensive. Do you have the budget to provide food, grooming supplies, veterinary care, and other basic needs for your pet? While deciding if you are ready for a pet, don't make impulsive decisions because you came across a cute animal and thought it would be easy to take care of. Instead, make your decision by being well educated, prepared, and committed to providing a pet with a loving and caring forever home.

Irresponsible:
There are cruel people in this world who get a pet, mistreat it, neglect it, and abandon it. They leave their pets out on the streets to fend for themselves and make excuses for their poor actions. Don't be one of these people, and treat animals with kindness.

Notice

This book went over general care for 28 pets. Some of these pets may require other needs than what is described in this book, so be sure to research and learn more about the pet you're interested in.

The End!

remember to:

Believe
Dream
Achieve

More Bearific books
on bearific.com

Katelyn Lonas

Katelyn is a 17 year old who resides in Southern California. Katelyn enjoys encouraging others to always believe in themselves and chase after their dreams! She began writing and illustrating her first book at age 9 and went on to publish 70 more books. She hopes you loved this book and are excited for more to come!

Katelyn Lonas

www.ingramcontent.com/pod-product-compliance
Lightning Source LLC
Chambersburg PA
CBHW042010080426
42734CB00002B/32